AF322660

DOLCE AMORE

Helle Gade

Title: Dolce Amore

Author: Helle Gade

Published by Butterdragons® Publishing

https://butterdragons.com

ISBN: 9789493229518 (ebook)

ISBN: 9789493229525 (hardback)

ISBN: 9789493229532 (audio book)

Cover Design by: Dazed Designs

Audio book narrated by Martha Webb

To my fellow poet Sonja Djurisevic. You are pure sunshine and I'm honoured to bask in your light.

For Helle, with love

She's always been a woman with a beautiful heart, so giving and loving. No one could say a bad word about her. Her body protested, the sickness making it hard for her to keep giving. The woman was brave and found a way to give more of her heart to those who needed it.

It started one day when she found an escape, one that was right before her eyes the whole time. Curling up in her bed with her furry princess by her side, she gave to the world beautiful, gripping words, ones that touched the soul. So many emotions poured from her hands, written in ink for all to enjoy. Every word a window to her beautiful soul. The pain, the love, the passion and darkness – all of it poured from her heart and onto the page. The words so touching and written so beautifully, her talent for giving life to emotions beyond compare.

When the pain was too much to bear, she picked up a book and found another answer, a way to give even more of herself. Losing herself in worlds full of danger, love, and adventure between the pages of books, she knew others would need the escape she had found. With such a huge heart, she gave that gift to others, sharing the love of the journeys she read, giving an escape from trauma and pain. Maybe she will never know how much her gift has changed the lives of all the people she touched, but she's a humble woman, continuing to do what she loves without a care for fortune or fame.

With her renewed passion, she found friends who shared her love of reading and appreciated her gifts more than she could have ever expected. Love in abundance came back to her but she'll never know how much she's loved and respected, relied upon by so many for an escape from their reality. Magic is her own passion, yet she doesn't know how magical she is on her own.

Her gift of the written word is one that transcends time, always to touch souls of generations to come long after those who have had the privilege to be a part of her world are gone.

by BDP Authors

The Price

We play
Then we pay
A steep price
Haunting
And
Painful
Yet
We do it again
And again
Hoping
This time
Will be different

My Love

Bringing my heart into the open
Is a frightful thing
When I have been hiding
In the trenches
Fiercely protecting it
For longer than can I remember

I expect a mortar attack
At any moment
Vaporising the frail organ
Leaving me to burrow deeper
Into the muddy trenches
To grow a new one

But hope pulls me forth
Whispering about freedom
And all-consuming love
Making me realise
That I have to chance it
To live to the fullest

Immortality

How can the moon and the stars be so far away
When I feel them etched into my soul?
Their light making me shine
Connecting me to the endless universe

Yet, I cannot touch them
My desperate desires
Warring within my very being
A deep profound sadness
Battling
With the glory of eternal light

I feel tiny like a grain of sand
Yet, immortality is lying at my feet

It is a circle of magic
It must be

Goodbye

You rouse me from my sleep
Gently placing a kiss on my lips
I see the truth in your eyes
That this is the final goodbye
The strings are cut
The emotions banished
All that is left is a lie
That you try to comfort me with

But I'm not that easily fooled
I want to kick and scream
To throw myself at your feet
And beg you to stay
But my pride stops me
I have to set you free
In the hopes that one day
You'll return to stay

Annihilation

You wear and tear my heart
Acting as if it's yours to demolish
Yours to take from my chest
Dropping it with casual carelessness

You command and demand
The submission of my soul
Bit by bit, you poison me
With cruel intent

As you burn and scatter
The being that is me
I let your words
Eat me up inside

I scream and fight
But the hold you have over me
Is stronger than steel
Darker than a starless night sky

Oh, how I mourn the loss of myself
Giving up on the hope
That life I dreamt in my younger years
Is still promised for my future

As I lie here broken
A shell of my former self
I apologize to myself continually
for letting it happen

Mother

Oh, sweet merciful mother
As I lay my head in your lap
My tears stain your apron

You stroke my hair
Whispering the words from your heart
Which is all I need to hear

They give me the courage to carry on
To raise my head high
And be the woman you raised me to be

Oh, sweet merciful mother...

Seasons

I mourn the fleeting heat of summer
Its escape towards the other side of the world
Drawn by tigers and prey alike

All that is left
Wolf's howling at the moon
Darkness to shadow my soul

I must fight my urge to hibernate
Sleeping through the winter and night
Hoping to wake when the snowbells bloom

Void

I allow myself to sink into the void
To release all tension
As I rest in the darkness

No words, just beautiful silence
Caressing my soul like a crisp winter morning
I feel myself throwing off the burden of living
At peace within myself

If only I could stay
In the warm embrace of ignorance
Forever afloat in peace

Lost Love

A flood of emotions
Tactile and tantalizing one minute
Pain-filled hatred the next
Warring against each other
Inside my skull
Trying to break through
To evaporate into thin air
Leaving me

Hollow
Cold

Longing for the sweet pain
Of the battlefield
That is empty now
Poppies flourishing
Where blood was spilled
During the fight of the century

Their red colour

A reminder of desperate passion

Tearing two people apart

In a futile attempt

To hold onto love

New Stars

The madness in their hearts
Ripped the Universe apart
In a cataclysmic explosion
Of rose petals and stardust

New life hesitantly emerged
In the light of old stars
Kissing the fragments
Of love and hatred

Conflicting emotions
Course through the system
Lighting the nerve endings
In a blazing inferno of hope

New dawn has broken
A myriad of colours
Creating a dream like vision
Asking all to breath anew

Joy

A whisper

Floating on gentle currents

A scent

Streaming in a fragrant mist

A memory

Rising to the surface

A feeling

Blossoming in my chest

A heart

Filling with love

A day

I remember with joy

Hanstholm

The first fall storm is upon us
The sea showing its teeth
Foam flying over the dunes
Sand grazing my skin
The scent of brine is strong
Bringing forth memories
Of years long gone
Of my grandmother and grandfather
The way we searched for amber
After every storm
Hoping to find the precious pieces
Laughing as we combed through
The rocky beach
My grandfather's whistling
Lost in the wind
As we made our way home
What a joy to enter the warm kitchen
Knowing homemade bread rolls
Were waiting for us all
After hours in the fresh sea air

Remembering my grandmother's
Bright red lipstick
And her perfume surrounding us
While she moved around the kitchen
Making sure that we were well fed
Those times are in the past
But every storm
Brings the memories back

Harvesting

Sweet summer nights

Sounds of farmers harvesting

The scent of it

Brings out childhood memories

Of helping my grandparents

Out in the field

Now, all I harvest is memories

And forgotten joys

Passion

A touch

A memory

Soft lips

A sigh

How I crave

Dream

A connection

Beyond hope

Painful longing

Unparalleled

Whispers

Honey laced words
Whispering over silk skin
A breath of brandy
Heating the blood
Shadow fingers dancing
Over sensitive flesh
A high so incredible
That she might never recover
Or in any way repay
Such love

Sigh

Captivate me with your dreams

Tell me stories of your adventurous deeds

Let me see behind the façade

Where you hide your true self

Let me add it all to my secrets

To the person I hide from the world

Hymn of Death

The trees move in the wind
My death song howling through the air
Making the leaves tremble
As if knowing of the violence to come

I slide through the underbrush
A silent shadow
Creeping vines follow in my wake
Towards the sacrificial alter

I hum the Hymn of Death
Drawing him to me
Like bees to honey
A promise of complete submission

I rejoice at the sight of him
In all his dark glory
Holding my winding cloth
In his skeleton hand

I accept and surrender to my fate
In the hands of this powerful creature
My mortality, now a faint memory
As I succumb to his fatal touch

A peace like no other surrounds me
As he enfolds me in his arms
I breathe out my gratitude
In a final peaceful exhalation

Tempest

How can I ever leave here
Turn my back to the grey blue ocean
The smell of brine in the air
A fierce wind caressing my face
My feet digging in the damp sand

How can I leave
When my heart tells me to stay
My soul flourishing in the wild storm
Dragging the breath from my lungs
Towards the tempest

Blind Love

My love was blind
My love was bloody

Obliterated by vile words
And malevolent actions

Loathing coats my skin
Slowly filling my lungs

Vengeful thoughts litter my mind
Seductive... Harsh.... Inviting...

I feel it slide under my skin
Divine intoxication filling my veins

Let me curse you
Devilish joy in making a decision

It will be the last you ever make
But it will be your best

Etchings

Beneath his rugged face
I find a dark space
Beneath those hidden fears
I find the tears
A mortal pain
Etched on his body
A celestial agony
Engraved on his soul

He smells of the ocean
On a stormy winter night
He feels like the northern wind
Sweeping over the country
His touch
A freezing breeze
His voice
A whisper of madness
One look
Bares my soul
One touch
Commands my body

Broken

There is no veil between me
And the unforgiving truth
The pain of it brings me to my knees

Heartbroken and lost
I fumble my way ahead
Blinded
By the twisted lies and promises

Take mercy on me
For I am a mere human
Broken by your words
Haunted and taunted by your lies

All that is left
Is a broken-down shell
And pain

Heart of Fire

Look to the waters below
Where the whales sing
And the current teases me

When the wind
And the wolves howl
I will be there
Right below the surface
Counting the stars

Look to the skies above
When the Eagle screams
And the clouds gather

I will be there
Pushing and pulling the sea
Illuminating the ocean

Look to the ground beneath

When the wind

And the wolves howl

I will be there

Absorbing the seeds

And pushing them towards the sky

Look to the heart of fire

I will be there

Muse

Darkness falls
And my muse appears
Pouring inspiration
Into my soul
A constant flow
In a wide spectrum
Of the human condition

I play with words
Filling them with emotion
Hoping they will lead others
To recognise a fellow traveller

I pour my heart out onto the page
Sharing my joys and fears
Pains and pleasures
In complete honesty
Thereby healing my soul
Bit by glorious bit
And perhaps show
That you are not alone

Everlasting Dreams

Take me down the road
Of everlasting dreams

Show me the wonders
Of humanity's fantasies

Daydreams in full bloom
Sleeping wishes

Simple thoughts we all carry with us
Consciously or unconsciously

Hopes and wishes
That live in our hearts and souls

The innermost desire
Fuelling our being

The reasons we fight
When all seems hopeless

You

You're all I ever think about

Night and day, you invade my thoughts

With no regard for my equilibrium

You waltz in and make a mess of me

I see your face, I feel your embrace

As I shudder and moan

Instantly regretting letting you go

But I had to do it

Before I broke

Before you tore me wide open

With your overflowing personality

That forced mine to retreat

To hide in the darkness

As you shone like the Sun

His Captive

His words are ash on my tongue
His touch acid on my skin

Peeling it from the bone
One strip at a time

He is my personal hell
That I cannot escape

My mind is a prison
My bars his hurtful actions

I have lost myself
To his evil ministrations

A captive
With no escape

Oxygen

You took my breath away
You stole it
When my eyes were blind
And my ears deaf
A thief in the night
Going for my precious gold
Siphoning from me
Every time I exhaled
Leaving my next breath shorter
Until my oxygen was low
And my body weak

Nebula

There's a tempest in my soul

Let it free, let it free

Sweep over me

Take me higher

Through the galaxy, I fly

On stardust and nebulous gases

To finally answer

What is my purpose?

Hurt

With your words you conditioned me
In the slipstream of every fight
The seed of manipulation
Was sown in my mind
Festering in my thoughts
Without my knowledge or consent

To this day, it strikes me
When I least expect it
Tearing down the confidence
That I have so carefully
Built over the years

The sores are ripped open
Pus oozes from them
Words of sickening control
Freezing me in place
Remembering lost innocence

Those days are long gone

My life is quite different now

I am stronger and wiser

Though never immune to the past

No matter how much I wish it

Nymph

It was a bright day
She went to dip her toe

Fate caught up to her
And she was dragged under

Ebb and flow
Caught her by surprise

The water burned in her throat
As life slowly left her body

But the truth was simpler
Neptune desired her

She reminded him
Of the sea during storm

Wild and carefree
A nymph in the making

Mine

Her

You will court me night and day
I'm your mistress
And I will master you as I wish
Taste the bite of my whip
As the punishment and reward
For you are mine, soul and body

Him

I am the sword in your hand
The light in your eyes
The fire that burns in your heart
The breath of life in your soul
I am yours to do with as you please
My heart is yours to crush or cradle

My Heart

I stretch my heart
To its very limits

But only in my dreams
Does it have free rein

In my waking hours
I guard it ferociously

Though I do not know why
Or how it happened

One day it was free
Now it's locked behind stonewall

Perhaps it is fear
For the great unknown

I wonder if there is anyone
Who can penetrate that stone

And embrace my heart
And the entirety of my soul

I dearly wish
That someone would come

As I fear terribly
For my heart slowly withering away

Like a flower without water
Left in the unrelenting sun

Gone

I hunger for your taste

For the smell

That clings to my sheets

The silken touch

Of your lips on my skin

I have come to crave

Your gentle

Yet firm touch

That made me feel

Loved

Safe

But I am denied

Your addictive presence

I chased you away

With my silence

And actions best left forgotten

How I yearn now
Wallowing in my misery
Alone with my cold heart
And empty emotions
Adrift in my own little world

How I need you
To melt my soul
And fight my indifference
To love and protect
My frail state of being

I need you

Loving Hope

A stolen moment
Beneath the apple blossoms
Sweet romance

Soon forgotten
In a wash of tears
Grim heartbreak

A gentle flutter
What is that feeling?
I dare again

Once more
I give away my love
Eternal hope

Goddess

She held the moon gently
Letting her fingers
Trail slowly
Over the mottled surface
Controlling the gravitational push and pull
Of Earth's great bodies of water
While the beasts of the forest
Howl their song of worship

Summer

My body and soul
Are missing summer
Like a dehydrated sailor
Surrounded by saltwater

I crave the gentle breeze
And the sun caressing
My skin with love
And tender kisses

I miss the colours
Of the flowers
Buzzing bees
And delicate butterflies

I yearn to walk below
The cool canopy of trees
Watching the dandelions
Sway and dance in the wind

Soon, I tell myself
Soon, spring will be here
Bringing tidings
Of the summer to come

Guide Me

Guide me into the golden light
Before the lightning strikes
And the thunder shakes the earth

Guide me into the heart of your home
Where it is warm and safe
Protecting us from the storm

Guide me into the bliss of love
Embrace me, body and soul
For I give myself freely to you

Guide me into the comfort
Of your body
Guide me into the comfort
Of your love

Blaze

Firestarter
Firestarter

Come, burn my house
Come, burn my soul

Firestarter
Firestarter

The raging inferno
Burns within you

Firestarter
Firestarter

Your flames lick my skin
They melt my resolve

Firestarter
Firestarter

You burn so bright
Your eyes alight

Firestarter
Firestarter

What have I done
To earn your wrath?

Firestarter
Firestarter

Come, feel my cool waters
Let me douse your flames

Firestarter
Firestarter

Burn big and bright
But don't burn my light

I See You

I see you
The true you
Never doubt that
The evil
Pouring out of you
Your eyes
Glowing orbs of hate

Oh, I see you
How could I not
When I am so often
The target
Letting your wrath
Sweep over me
A dark cloud
Full of burning needles
Hammering
At my thin shields

I definitely see you

Despite the fact

That you are

A brilliant actor

Fooling most people

But not me

Never me

Northern Pride

The Northman's song
Of wind and light

Of green fields
And sacred hills

Of ancient oak forests
And the hidden people

Of western beaches
And fall storms

Of Vikings, wolves
And the old gods

Of belonging
And family

Of the old ways
To which we belong

Black Sun

Black sun
Here I come

Burning a bright trail
Of my past behind

Looking towards the sky
With a soul-deep longing

One step more
And I'll begin anew

Night

The night is my lover

At times, it excites me

At times, it calms me

One thing is for sure

It never fails me

No matter how strong

The sun is during daytime

The night will fall

And shroud me in darkness

The gentle silver light of the moon

And stars dotting the sky

Is the only light that guides me

Through wilderness of my emotions

And offers a retreat after a hectic day

Beginnings

Soft, wavy hair
Running through my fingers
I tug at it gently
Bringing those soft lips closer
To taste and feel them

I want your breath
I want your passion
To be one with you
As our souls merge

I want you despite
And because of your flaws
I'll take your baggage
And place it next to mine
As we settle in for the long haul

La Luna

The moon prowls
Across the sky
Sometimes hidden
Behind silken clouds
But always a cool
Silver presence
Surrounded
By thousands of stars
Like a jewelled
Studded cape
The Milky Way
A diamond necklace
Gracing
The Lunar Goddess
As she watches
Over the children
That haunt
A sleepless night

Delicious Sin

Cover me in the night
A velvet blanket
Sensual and mysterious
Forbidden secrets
Hiding in the shadows
The ecstasy of sin
Waiting beyond the light

I dare you
To enter the darkness
And show me
Who you truly are
To share your wickedness
With the fallen angels
Waiting in the dark

Alien

His eyes were blank
Like a mirror surface
Yet, no reflection showed

Those unfathomable orbs
Gazed into my very core
Searing through me

May your soul shatter
For the pain inflicted on me
The heartache you caused me

I know those words are feeble
They will not affect you
They will not make you stop

You have no mercy to give
No understanding
Of my humanity

I Wish

I wish to be the cool moon
In the darkness
Which you gaze upon
As you rest for the night

I wish to be the dawn
That wakes you
From your slumber

I wish to be your sun
To be the heat
That sustains you

I wish to be the dusk
That reminds you
That it is time
To rest in my arms

I wish to be the stars

That are reflected

In your eyes

As you gaze upon me

Yellow Leaf

I sway high over the countryside

Carried by the northern wind

Towards the shores unknown

I herald the end of a season

And the beginning of winter storms

Eventually

I will land

I will decompose

And become part of the earth

On which the snowdrop breaks

Again

I herald the end of a season

And the return of starlings and sunshine

Acknowledgements

To Ira and Sonja for helping me make sense of the chaos I make. I couldn't have done it without you ladies. Love you!

I have to thank Tash from Dazed Design for the gorgeous cover. You are absolutely amazing!!!!

Thank you dear readers for taking a chance and reading my book.

About Helle Gade

Helle Gade lives in Denmark with her little diva dog. She is a book blogger, poet, photographer, nocturnal creature, avid reader and chocolate addict. She has been writing poetry since 2011 and published four poetry collections since then. She has been fortunate to work with a bunch of brilliant authors and photographers on The Mind's Eye series. Her book Nocturnal Embers won the Best Poetry Collection with eFestival of Words.

Other BDP books by Helle Gade

Terrifying Love - A Halloween Anthology

Beautiful Tragedy - A Halloween Anthology

How To Tame A Wild Tempest

Poesi - A Collection of Poems Volume One

The Fighter